14X 6/01 ✓8/01
27x 2/09 ✓10/09

D0601903

A Tribute to
THE YOUNG AT HEART

MARK TWAIN

By Jill C. Wheeler

Published by Abdo & Daughters, 4940 Viking Drive, Suite 622, Edina, Minnesota 55435.

Copyright © 1996 by Abdo Consulting Group, Inc., Pentagon Tower, P.O. Box 36036, Minneapolis, Minnesota 55435 USA. International copyrights reserved in all countries. No part of this book may be reproduced in any form without written permission from the publisher.

Printed in the United States.

Cover Photo credit: Bettmann Archives
Interior Photo credits: Bettmann Archives

Edited by Julie Berg

Library of Congress Cataloging-in-Publication Data

Wheeler, Jill C., 1964
    Mark Twain / Jill C. Wheeler.
    p. cm. — (Young at heart)
Summary: A biography of a great American humorist who had also been a printer, steamboat captain, news reporter, gold miner, and lecturer in a white linen suit.
ISBN 1-56239-519-X
1. Twain, Mark, 1835-1910—Biography—Juvenile literature. 2. Authors, American—19th century—Biography—Juvenile literature. [1. Twain, Mark, 1835-1910. 2. Authors, American.]
I. Title. II. Series: Tribute to the young at heart.
PS1331.W47   1995
818'.409—dc20
[B]   95-4664
                                               CIP
                                               AC

TABLE OF CONTENTS

THE MOST FAMOUS MAN IN AMERICA

It was winter 1906. A crowd had gathered at the famous Carnegie Hall. The evening was a special event to raise money for Booker T. Washington. He was an African American who helped other African Americans get an education. People lined up to hear that evening's speaker. It was a man called Mark Twain.

In 1906, Mark Twain was one of the most famous men in America. Many people had read his letters and novels. He also loved to speak in public and tell stories. Wherever he was, a crowd was sure to follow. The man in the white linen suit, for which Twain was known, was a popular personality.

Mark Twain was born Samuel Langhorne Clemens on November 30, 1835, in the small town of Florida, Missouri. Samuel was the fifth child of John and Jane Clemens. That same day, Halley's Comet was visible in the night sky. Star gazers can see the comet from Earth only once every 75 years.

Mark Twain was one of the most famous men in America during the 19th century.

Samuel's mother once said he was special—in an unusual way. "You gave me more uneasiness than any child I had," she told him. "I suppose you were afraid I wouldn't live," he answered. "No, afraid you would," she joked back.

Samuel loved jokes of any kind. He also had a talent for telling funny stories. Friends said he was so funny he could make anyone laugh. Samuel used his talents throughout his life. He entertained people with his lectures, letters, books and stories. Much of his material came from his own childhood in Hannibal, Missouri. Hannibal sits on the shores of the mighty Mississippi River.

Behind Samuel's laughter was a serious side. He constantly fought against injustice. He deeply believed in equality for African Americans. He felt people should treat each other better. He used his writings and lectures to remind people of their responsibilities to each other. His humor reminded them of how unfair and silly they could be.

JOKES, PRANKS AND STORIES

No one loved a good joke as much as Samuel Clemens. He also loved to play tricks on people. He often got into trouble because of it. When he was young, he put snakes in his aunt's sewing basket. He hid bats in his pockets for his mother to find. He dropped a watermelon shell on his brother's head from three stories above him. He even faked being hypnotized on several occasions as a joke.

Samuel attended a one-room log schoolhouse. He didn't enjoy most of his classes, but he did like spelling and history. He often won the school's weekly spelling bee. In spite of his spelling success, he had some problems with his teacher, Mrs. Horr. "I broke one of the rules and was told that the penalty for a second breach was a whipping," he wrote later. "I presently broke the rule again and Mrs. Horr told me to go out and find a switch and fetch it." For the switch, Samuel found a tiny, rotten piece of wood he knew would not hurt him.

Mrs. Horr quickly sent another student to find a different and better switch.

Outside of school, Samuel had a partner for many of his tricks. His name was Tom Blankenship. Tom could come and go as he pleased. He lived in a shed behind Samuel's house. Late at night, Tom and Samuel would sneak away on adventures. Sometimes they dug for buried treasure. Samuel later modeled his character Huck Finn after Tom.

Once Samuel and some other friends rolled a huge boulder down a hill near Hannibal. The boulder almost crashed into a horse and wagon. Instead, it smashed into a barrel shop. Some people thought Samuel Clemens would never amount to anything but a troublemaker.

Samuel's parents were just glad he was alive. He had been very sick as a baby. His mother had given him bottles of castor oil to make him better. In those days, many babies died before their first birthday. Many others died before their twenties. Before he was ten, Samuel lost a brother and a sister to disease.

Mark Twain visiting his boyhood home, Hannibal, Missouri, in 1902.

Hannibal, at one time, had a measles outbreak. His parents kept Samuel home so he would not catch the disease. They were afraid he would die if he caught it. Samuel wanted to get sick to find out if he would live or die. He visited a friend who had measles so he could catch them. He did get sick, but he lived.

A highlight for Samuel during those years was his summer trips. He visited relatives on a farm near his birthplace. There he enjoyed wonderful Southern-style cooking and plenty of room to play. He also liked to visit the slaves on his relatives' farm. He spent hours listening to the slaves tell stories. It was here he learned to love stories and to tell them well.

AN APPRENTICE PRINTER

When Samuel was only eleven, his father died. His family became very poor. Samuel had to get a job. His older brother, Orion, worked at a newspaper in St. Louis. Samuel thought that sounded interesting. He got a job as an apprentice for two years at a Hannibal newspaper. He received no money, just a promise. He would get a place to stay, food, and two suits each year.

At the newspaper, Samuel learned how to set type and run the printing press. When his apprenticeship was over, he went to work for Orion. Orion had come back to Hannibal and was running another newspaper. When Orion went out of town, Samuel wrote the newspaper articles. He enjoyed that. Some of his articles got Orion into trouble. Samuel liked to take the news and make it more interesting. What he wrote wasn't always true. Not everyone wanted to read what he had to say.

Samuel also began writing stories about life in Hannibal. When he was fifteen, he sent some stories to magazines. Several magazines published his work. His writing career had begun.

Samuel found it hard to work with Orion. Sometimes they disagreed. Soon he decided he was ready to go out on his own. He looked for a printing job in St. Louis. After that, he went to Philadelphia and then New York. He would stay in one place long enough to see the town and earn some money. Then he would leave. Between jobs, he wrote his family colorful letters describing his experiences.

Samuel traveled this way for more than a year. When he returned to Hannibal, Orion had gone. He had moved to Iowa to work at a newspaper office. Samuel decided to join him.

Samuel soon found Iowa boring. As he always had, he read many books. One was about the Amazon in South America. He decided he wanted to go there. After finding a fifty-dollar bill, he booked passage on a steamboat. He was going to South America.

When Samuel landed in New Orleans, he learned no boats were going to the Amazon soon. That didn't matter though. He had found a new love during his trip to New Orleans—steamboats.

CAPTAIN CLEMENS

Like the other boys in Hannibal, steamboats fascinated Samuel. Many were beautiful and glamorous. The people on them appeared to lead more exciting lives than anyone in Hannibal. Plus, everyone treated the steamboat pilots well. They made lots of money.

Horace Bixby captained Samuel's boat to New Orleans. For $500, Horace agreed to teach Samuel how to be a pilot. Samuel became a cub pilot. He spent two years traveling up and down the Mississippi. He learned every inch of the river. He knew how deep the water was in different places. He learned the location of sunken logs and sandbars. He could tell where the boat was day and night.

Samuel loved piloting so much he encouraged his younger brother Henry to become a pilot. Henry did. One night Samuel dreamt he saw Henry in a coffin with a red rose on his chest. Later, the boat Henry was on blew up. Henry died after the explosion. When Samuel saw Henry's body, it was just like in his dream.

From then on, supernatural events fascinated him. In 1859, Samuel got his pilot's license. Captain Clemens was a favorite with his passengers. They loved to listen to his slow drawl. They laughed at his stories. In fact, Samuel said later he loved to be "killingly" funny. Meanwhile, he made $250 a month, which was a lot of money.

This steamboat on the Mississippi River was much like the one Mark Twain piloted.

Each day, Samuel heard the crew speaking the language of steamboats. There were many terms that had special meanings to river crews. One term was "mark twain." It meant that the water was deep enough for the boat to pass safely. Crews would throw a rope into the water to see how deep it was. If it was at least twelve feet deep, they would yell out "mark twain!" He never forgot that term.

Samuel loved life on the river. Unfortunately, the Civil War cut his career short. When the war began, boats could no longer travel freely. People didn't have the money to go anywhere either. Samuel had to quit his job. He spent several weeks as a Confederate soldier. Then he decided he did not like being a soldier.

Samuel returned to Iowa. When he got there, Orion told him he had a new job. He was going to be the assistant to the governor of the Nevada territory. However, he didn't have the money to get to Nevada. Could Samuel help?

WEST TO SEEK A FORTUNE

Samuel took money from his piloting days and bought passage to Nevada for both of them. They arrived in Carson City after nineteen days on a stagecoach.

The wild American West excited Samuel. He had heard many stories about prospectors finding gold and silver. A man could become rich overnight. Samuel tried his hand at mining. In December 1861, he set out with some friends to seek his fortune. He spent a year looking for riches. He also found time to write letters about his adventures. He sent the letters to a newspaper in Virginia City, Nevada. The newspaper published them. People loved to read Samuel's letters.

Eventually, the newspaper offered Samuel a job as a reporter. He would make $25 a week. That was more money than he had made from prospecting. He accepted the job. Since he didn't have the money to travel to Virginia City, he walked there.

As before, Samuel "improved" the news he covered. Sometimes he even made up stories and called them news. He made up a story about finding a petrified prospector in Nevada. Many people believed him. Yet the story was false. Samuel also began signing the name Mark Twain to his writings.

It wasn't long before Samuel's writing got him in trouble again. He was ordered to leave Nevada. He went to California. He tried mining for gold once again. But he found nothing. During that time, he wrote a funny story. He called it "The Celebrated Jumping Frog of Calaveras County." Newspapers around the country printed his story. People began noticing Mark Twain.

Now the writing bug had really bitten Samuel. He convinced a newspaper in California to send him to Hawaii. In those days, people called Hawaii the Sandwich Islands. Samuel sent back stories about his adventures there. His stories told about steaming volcanoes and lush plantations. While he was in Hawaii, there was a terrible shipwreck. The ship was called the *Hornet*. Samuel interviewed the survivors.

He nearly missed talking to them. He had saddle sores from riding horses and could barely move. People had to carry him on a stretcher to the interviews. Samuel laid on the stretcher while he took notes.

After the interviews, he wrote a thrilling story. He called it "Forty-Three Days in an Open Boat." He sold it to a popular magazine. Unfortunately, the editor couldn't read Samuel's handwriting. He printed the story under the byline of Mark Swain.

INTRODUCING MARK TWAIN

Samuel made sure Mark Twain became a household word. He began giving lectures to earn money. These were humorous talks people paid to hear. His first lecture was in San Francisco in 1866. He had the crowd laughing almost the entire time. The lecture began his reputation as an outstanding public speaker.
Samuel's next project was a book. He put together a

collection of his stories and sent it to a publisher. Although the book did not sell many copies, Samuel was not ready to give up. He thought of a new assignment. He would travel to Europe and the Holy Lands and write about his experiences.

He left on a boat with a tour group in the summer of 1867. Most of the tourists were older and conservative. They gave Samuel lots of material for his letters. His publisher edited the letters and made them into a book, *The Innocents Abroad*. The book was Samuel's first major success.

In addition to the book, Samuel's journey led to another success. On the boat, he met a young man named Charles Langdon. Charles showed Samuel a portrait of his sister Olivia. Samuel couldn't get the portrait out of his mind. More than anything, he wanted to meet Olivia.

He got his chance in December when the tour boat returned to New York City. He took Olivia to hear author, Charles Dickens speak.

Livy, as he called her, impressed Samuel. Samuel did not impress Livy quite as much. It took him more than a year to convince her to marry him.

Livy and Samuel were married February 2, 1879. They moved to Buffalo, New York. There they lived in a beautiful new home Livy's father had given them. Samuel said he was "the happiest man on earth." His happiness spilled over into his career. The next years would bring him even more success as a writer and speaker.

TOM, BECKY, HUCK AND COMPANY

Samuel now had a contract to write ten pages of humor a month for a popular magazine. He also had been asked to write a book about his experiences out West. He did, and *Roughing It* was born. The book told of Samuel's experiences seeking a fortune in Nevada and California. Like his last book, readers loved *Roughing It*.

Soon the Clemens family moved to Hartford, Connecticut. There they built a new home. It was the most elaborate house in the city. It had nineteen rooms, eighteen fireplaces and five bathrooms. The front porch looked like a steamboat. Samuel's room featured a huge black bed with angels carved on it. The bed was big enough for a whole family.

In the summer, the Clemens went to Quarry Farm near Elmira, New York. It was Livy's sister's home. Livy had a special room built at the farm. It had eight sides, all lined with windows. Samuel spent many hours in the room writing. He worked on a new book based on his childhood experiences in Hannibal.

Twain wrote the beloved children's book, *The Adventures of Tom Sawyer.*

Sometimes he would write fifty pages a day. The main character in the new book was a boy named Tom Sawyer.

Back in Hartford, Samuel had another special room in which to write. It was at the top of his house. It looked like the pilothouse on a steamboat. There he completed *The Adventures of Tom Sawyer*.

The book had taken him more than two years to write. As with all his books, Livy was his editor. She would cross out anything she didn't like with a pencil. It became a game with Samuel to argue with her suggestions. Sometimes he wrote passages he did not want included just to see if she would cross them out.

At first, Samuel was not fond of Tom Sawyer. "It is not a boy's book at all," he wrote a friend. "It will only be read by adults." Samuel had no idea how wrong he was. The book was published in December 1876. It was an instant hit. Readers couldn't get enough of the adventures of Tom, Becky and Huck.

Samuel decided to begin writing a sequel. The sequel became *The Adventures of Huckleberry Finn*. Yet the writing was not going well. Samuel took a break and traveled with his family to Europe. He and Livy now had two daughters, Susy and Clara. They spent a year and a half in Europe. Samuel worked on two new books.

When the family returned home, Samuel published the new books. One was about his recent travels in Europe. The other was *The Prince and the Pauper*, about two boys who switch lives. It is one of his most famous books. The same year, he and Livy had a third daughter, Jean. It seemed nothing could go wrong for Samuel Clemens.

FORTUNES WON AND LOST

It was no secret that Samuel had a lot of money. Many people asked him to invest in their inventions. Sometimes he did. In 1880, he invested hundreds of thousands of dollars in a typesetting machine. As a young man, he had spent many hours setting type by hand. The machine's inventor said it would set type faster than any person.

As he waited for his investment to pay off, Samuel wrote another book. It was a collection of stories about life on the Mississippi. When that was done, he went back to *The Adventures of Huckleberry Finn*. More than any other book, Huck Finn reflected Samuel's own experiences.

Samuel chose to have Huck Finn published by his own new publishing company in 1884. For the company's second book, he wanted to publish a piece by Ulysses S. Grant. Grant had led the Union Army in the Civil War. The book came out after Grant had died. Samuel worked hard to make sure it was a success. He wanted Grant's widow to have plenty of money. Thanks to Samuel, she received more than $400,000.

The following years brought a string of misfortunes to the Clemens household. Samuel's investment in the typesetting machine still had not paid off. His publishing company began losing money. His mother died.

Samuel's fortune was slipping away. Thinking it was cheaper to live in Europe, Samuel moved his family there. They lived in Europe for several years. Then Samuel's publishing company went bankrupt. Samuel didn't have to pay all of his company's bills himself. However, he felt it was his duty. As before, he lectured to make more money.

Life on the road was hard. Livy and Clara went with Samuel. Susy and Jean stayed behind. Samuel spoke to packed houses wherever he went. People admired him for working so hard to pay off his debts. He started traveling west through the United States. Then he went to Hawaii, Australia, New Zealand, India and Africa. It took a year and a half.

Livy and Samuel planned to meet Susy and Jean in England. Weeks went by, yet Susy and Jean still had not arrived. Then they heard Susy was sick. Livy and Clara headed back across the ocean to be with her. Samuel stayed to find a place for the family to live when they were together again. They never were. Three days later, Susy died.

For the next five years, Samuel, Livy and their remaining children traveled around Europe. They tried to put Susy's death behind them. It was very hard. Samuel forced himself to write another book about his recent world tour. The money from that book paid off his remaining debts.

MORE! MORE!

The Clemens family returned to the United States in 1900. People greeted them warmly. By now, Samuel Clemens was the greatest American humorist ever.

Samuel delighted in the attention. He loved performing and liked to hear himself talk. He wasn't happy unless he dominated a conversation. Happily for him, people hung on his every word. Reporters often asked him for his opinion on something. He was always glad to give it.

Samuel once said he felt like "the most conspicuous person on the planet." Even though he complained, he loved the attention. Many people considered him the most photographed person in the world. Certainly, he was popular. There was even a Mark Twain impersonator working in Australia.

The Clemens family settled in New York. Samuel gave lectures again. Yet it wasn't long before people realized Samuel had changed. The new Samuel was still funny. Only this time, his humor had a message.

Samuel spoke out about social injustices. His comments made people laugh. They also made them think about things like crime, wars and racism. At the same time, he had other things on his mind. Livy always had been sickly. Now she was getting worse.

Livy died in June 1904. After thirty-four years of marriage, Samuel had lost his favorite and most beloved companion. Shortly after that, his sister Pamela died. It was a long time before he wrote again.

RETURN OF THE COMET

For the next three years, Samuel worked on his autobiography with another writer, Albert Paine. Paine had a hard job. Samuel had made up stories for so long, Paine spent much time sorting fact from fiction.

Between his work with Paine, Samuel played pool, his favorite game. He continued to receive some visitors and lots of fan mail. "I can live for two months on a good compliment," he said once.

Around 1906, Samuel began wearing his trademark white linen suit. He would have his tailor make six suits at a time. He liked white because it made him feel "clean in a dirty world." He also had his shirts custom-made with the buttons in the back. Once, he tried on three shirts in a row. Each had a button missing. He threw all three out the window and screamed loudly enough to wake his neighbors.

In December 1909, Samuel suffered another blow. His youngest daughter died of an epileptic seizure just before Christmas. Her funeral was held Christmas Day. After she died, Samuel found the Christmas gift she had for him. It was a globe, which he had always wanted.

Four months after Jean's death, Halley's Comet returned to the skies above America. It was the same comet that had visited when Samuel was born. Now, seventy-five years later, it visited on April 20, 1910—the day Samuel Clemens died.

Halley's Comet, April 20, 1910.

Thousands of people filed past his casket before the funeral. An entire nation mourned his death. Samuel Clemens had left a permanent imprint.

Another great American novelist, Ernest Hemingway, praised Samuel. "All modern American literature comes from ... Huckleberry Finn," he said. Many people believe *The Adventures of Huckleberry Finn* is America's greatest novel. Some people have wanted to ban the book because of how it portrays African Americans. They also say Huck Finn did not have morals. The debate rages to this day.

The Adventures of Huckleberry Finn is still in print, and will be for a long, long time. As for Samuel Clemens and Mark Twain, those names will forever be part of American history and culture.

GLOSSARY OF TERMS

Amazon — a giant South American river and the jungle around it.

Apprentice — a person learning a craft under a skilled worker.

Bankrupt — when a person or company runs out of money and cannot pay bills.

Breach — to break a rule or a law.

Castor Oil — a thick yellowish oil that is supposed to make people healthier.

Civil War — a conflict in American history between the Northern and Southern states over slavery.

Commune — a place where all residents own and share everything.

Confederate — of or belonging to the Confederacy, a group of eleven Southern States that left the United States in 1860 and 1861.

Conservative — a person who acts cautiously

Conspicuous — something that attracts attention.

Contract — a written agreement.

Cub — a young person in a particular field.

Epileptic Seizure — a sudden attack caused by the disease epilepsy.

Holy Lands — the places mentioned in Bible stories.

Humorist - A humorous talker; a writer of funny jokes and stories.

Hypnotized — to put someone into a deep sleep so they respond to suggestions.

Impersonate— to pretend to be.

Petrify— to turn into stone or a substance like stone.

Prospectors — people who looked for gold and silver to become rich.

Racism — to think some people are better than others because of their skin color.

Sequel — a book or movie that continues a story started in an earlier book or movie.

Slave — a person held as property and forced to work without pay.

Supernatural — something that has to do with things outside of nature, such as a ghost.

Switch — a tree branch used like a whip.

Union — the name of the Northern army in the Civil War.